Another Book

About Design

Complicated Doesn't Make It Bad

Mark Gonyea

Henry Holt and Company   New York

Henry Holt and Company, LLC
Publishers since 1866
175 Fifth Avenue
New York, New York 10010
www.henryholtchildrensbooks.com

Library of Congress Cataloging-in-Publication Data
Gonyea, Mark.
Another book about design : complicated doesn't make it bad / Mark Gonyea.
p.   cm.
ISBN-13: 978-0-8050-7576-2 / ISBN-10: 0-8050-7576-3
1. Design—Juvenile literature. I. Title.
NK1510.G578 2007   745.4—dc22   2006043705

First Edition—2007
Printed in China on acid-free paper. ∞

1   3   5   7   9   10   8   6   4   2

This book is
dedicated to my
favorite shape,
the circle.

*Just because it
looks complicated
doesn't mean it is.*

Chapter 1

The Big Picture

Every design begins
with a foundation to build on—
the Big Picture.

Once you have that,
everything else is just details.

No matter how much
you add . . .

. . . and add . . .

. . . and add . . .

. . . you always have the Big Picture
underneath it all.

Chapter 2

Down in Front!

The foreground in a design
is what's closest to you.

The background is, well, *in back*, away from you.

The red circle is most important
because it's in the foreground
and in front of the yellow squares.

If you bring the background forward,
then it becomes the foreground
and most important.

Chapter 3

Same but Different

"Same but different"
can provide an unlimited number
of variations on a single design.

Take the design to the right,
for example.

Same design.

Different color.

Again, same design.

Different colors.

Yet again, same design.
Different color.

Should I go on?
OK, if you insist!

Same design.
Different shapes.

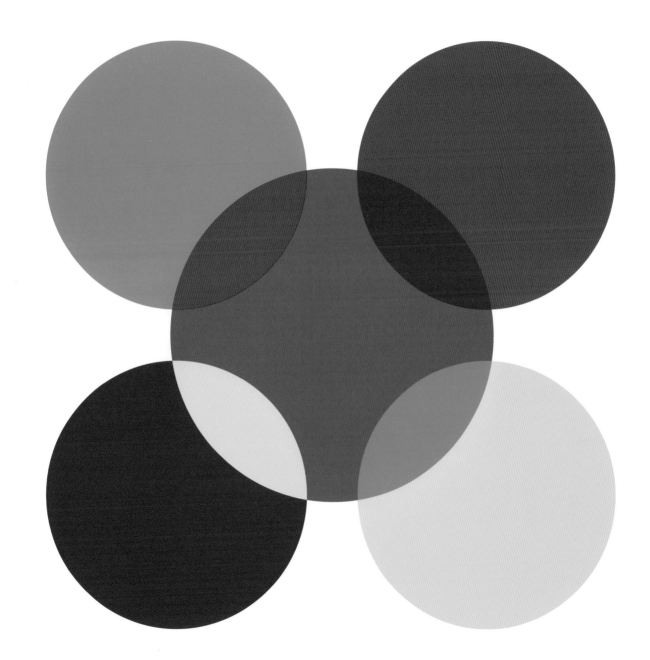

Same colors.
Different placement.

More? You're the boss!

Same design.

Same colors.

Different size.

Same design.
Same colors.
Different size.
Different amount.

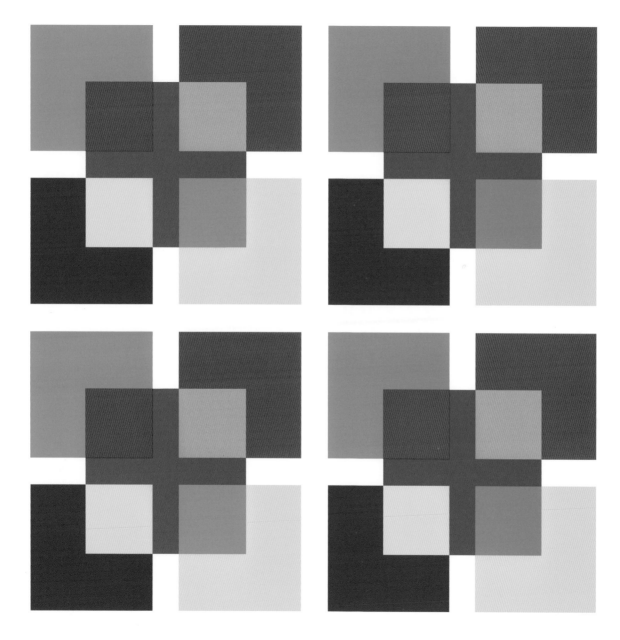

Same design.
Different colors.

We should probably
move on. Oh, OK, one more!

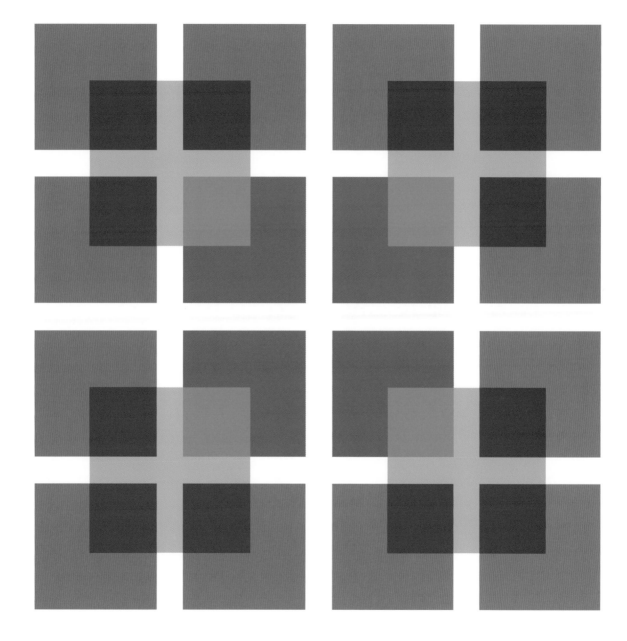

Same design.

Different colors.

Different placement.

Now we really need to move on.
Later, see how many different
variations you can do.

Chapter 4

Two for the Price of One

OK, stay with me now.

Each design element is everything it is and everything it is not.

That's called positive and negative space.

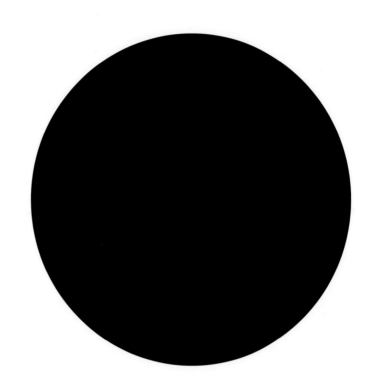

When you create one thing,
like this dot, you are actually
creating two things—
the dot and
the area around the dot.

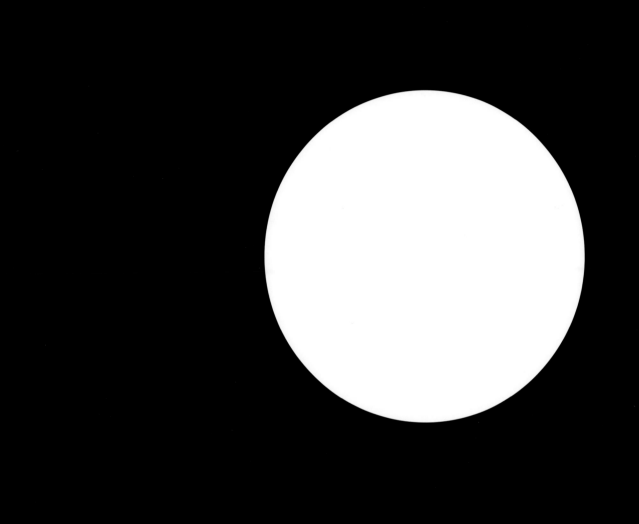

Negative space is
everything that's
not positive space . . .

. . . and positive space
is everything that's
not negative space.

You can't have one
without the other.

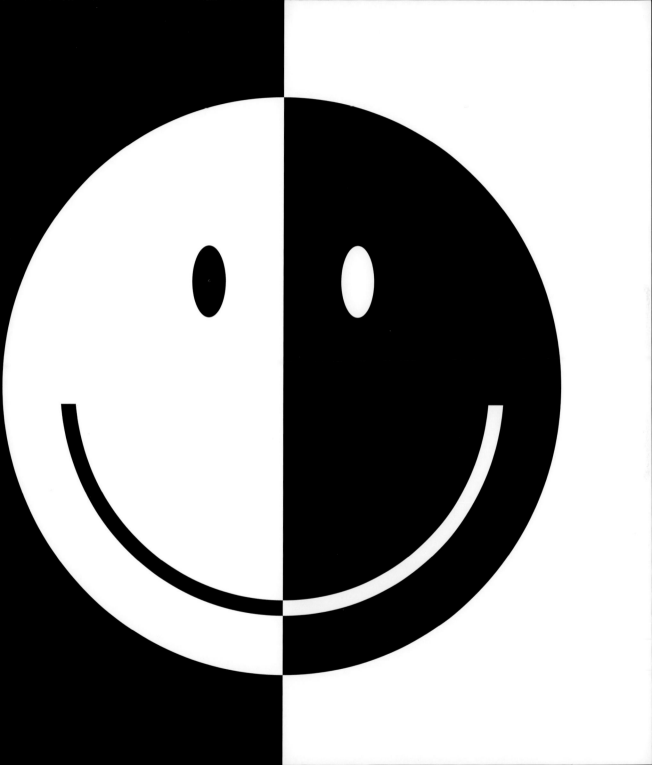

Chapter 5

Don't Stand
So Close to Me

Every element in a design
has personal space.
Too far apart
and tension is lost.

Too close and
even a simple design
seems crowded.

Keeping personal space in mind,
where would you place another dot
on this green page?

Here?

Sorry, try again.

How about here?

Nope.

Picture personal space
as a group of physical elements
to be avoided and worked around.

Bingo!

Chapter 6

I'm Not Complex—
There's Just More
of Me to Love

Alone, one square
is not very complicated.

Four sides. Four corners.
Pretty simple, right?

Multiply that simple shape
and you get a more complex design.

The more shapes you add,

the more complex the pattern.

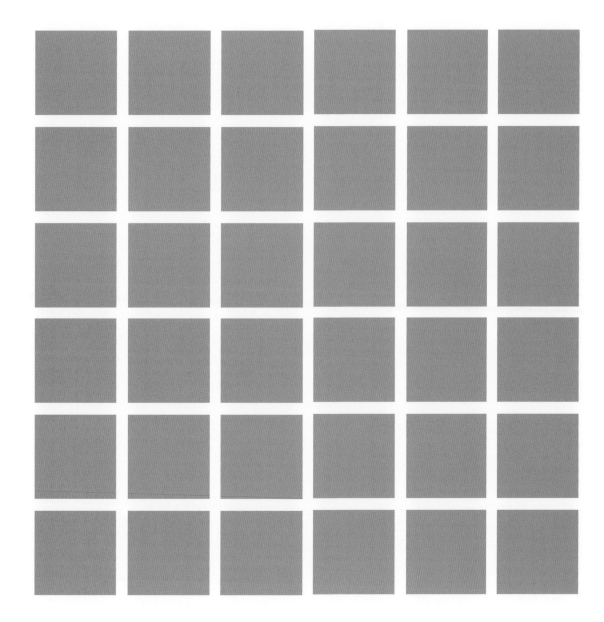

Sometimes many smaller
shapes can have more impact
than just one larger shape.

Like so!

Chapter 7

Squares Are from Mars, Circles Are from Venus

Circles are round.

Squares are not.

Circles are soft.

Squares are hard.

Circles are light.

Squares are heavy.

Circles are high.

Squares are low.

Circles can move you.

But squares can
stop you.

Chapter 8

Like Shapes? Me Too!

Similar elements can create
a sense of unity in a design.

Be it similar shapes . . .

. . . similar colors . . .

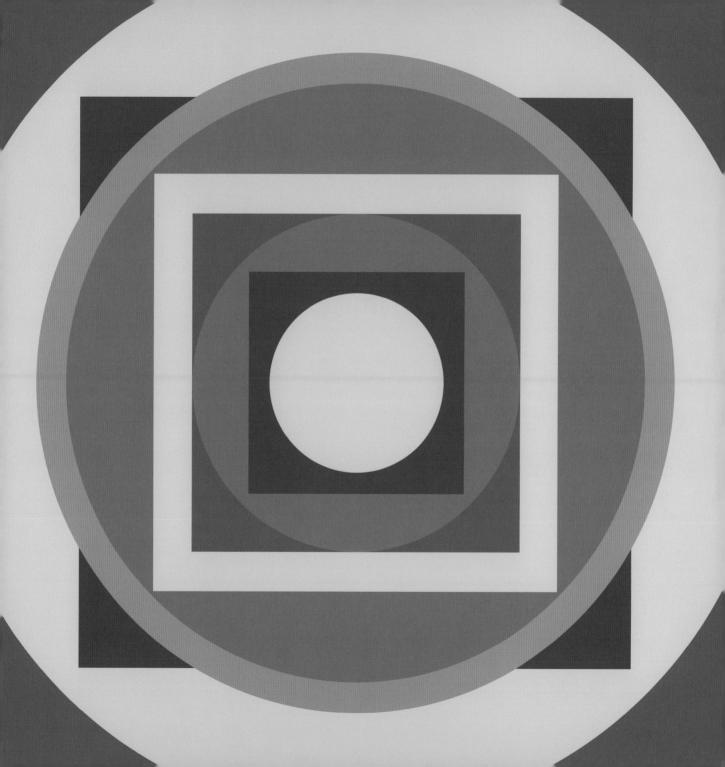

. . . or similar sizes.

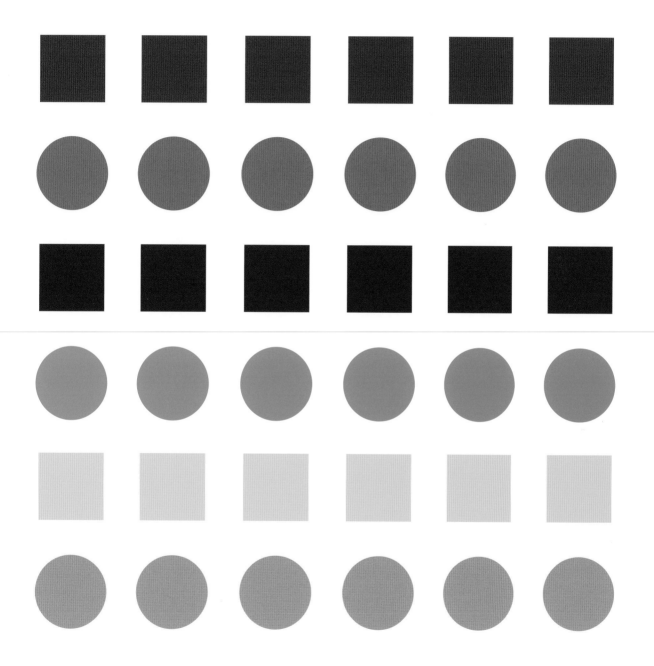

Similar curved cool shapes
create an impression
of tranquility and calmness . . .

. . . while similar jagged warm shapes
can give an impression
of action and excitement.

Chapter 9
Knock, Knock

Who's there?

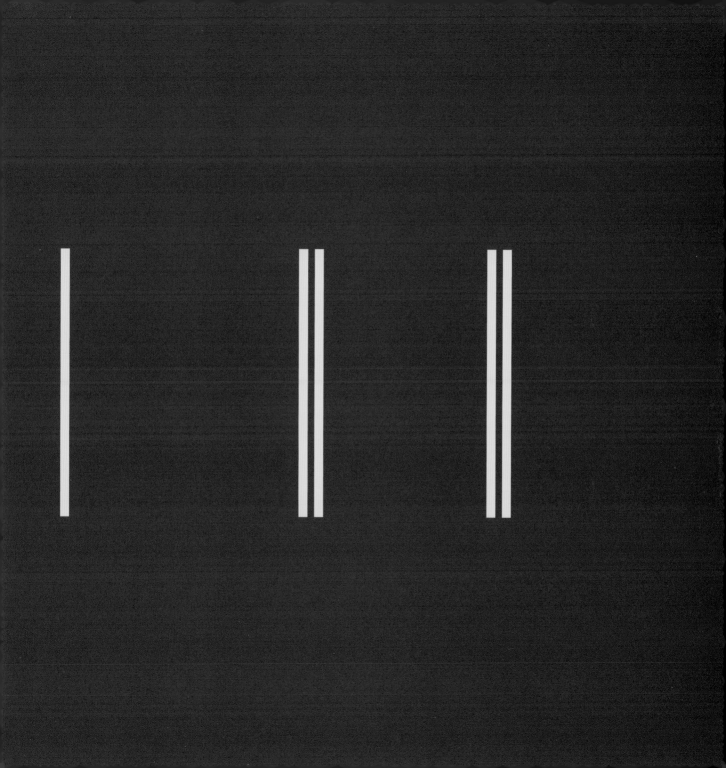

Line.

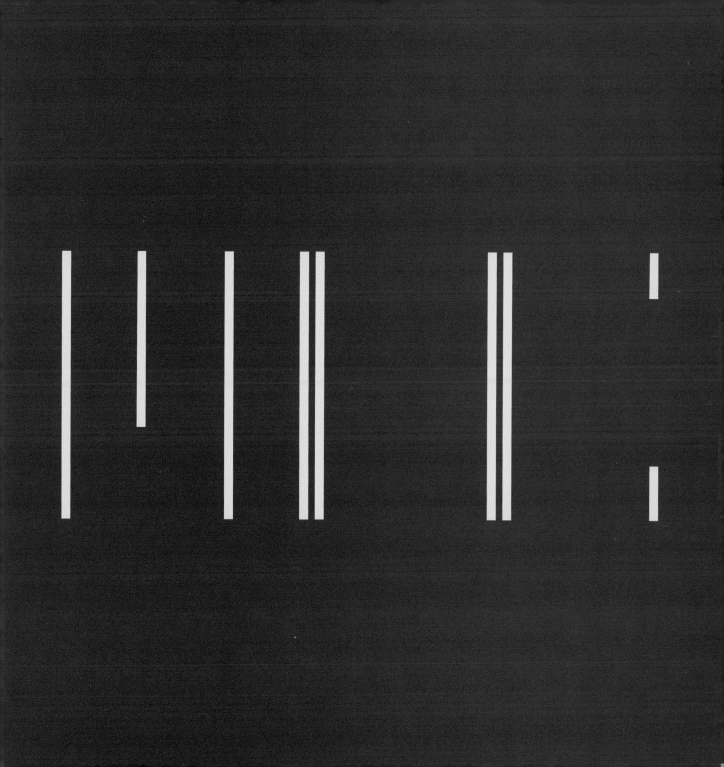

Line who?

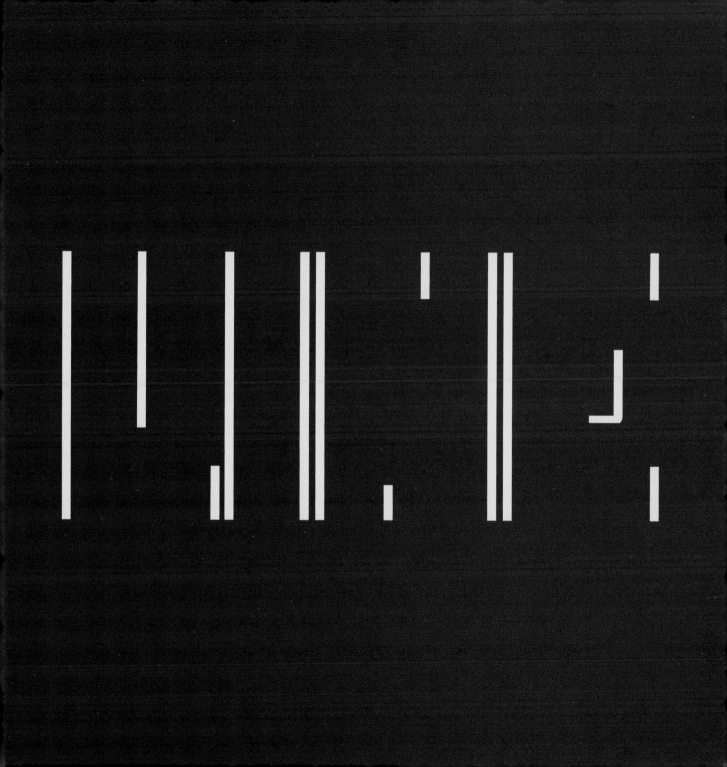

Lines are used
to help define shapes.

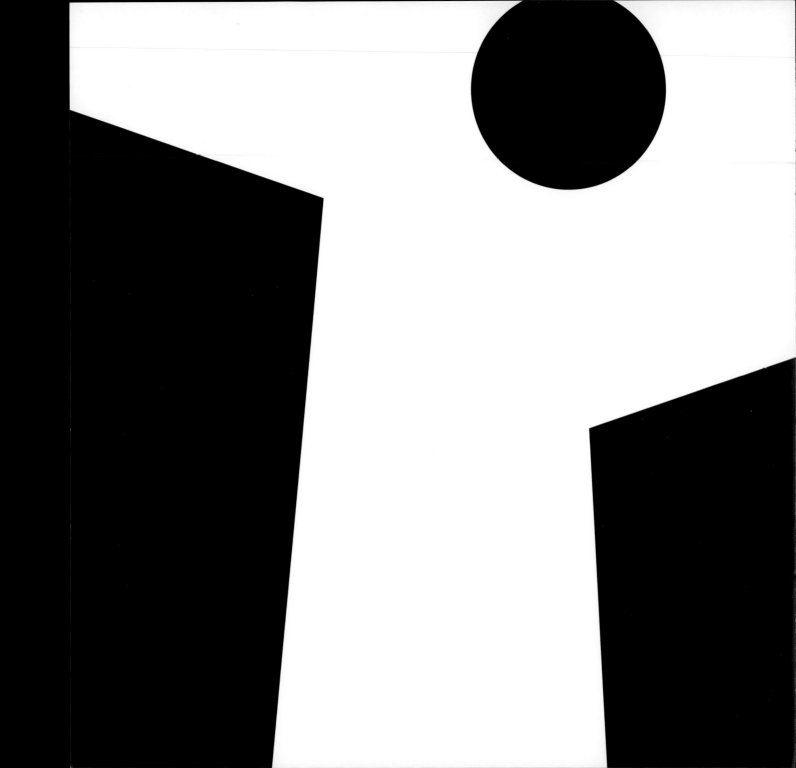

Chapter 10
Putting It Together

The Big Picture.

Background.

Positive and
negative space.

Personal space.

Circles are high.

Squares are hard.

The more shapes you add,
the more complex the pattern.

Add detail.

Same design.
Different colors.

Similar colors
create unity.

The foreground is
more important than
the background.

Lines are used
to help define shapes.

Similar jagged shapes
give an impression
of action and excitement.

Just because
it looks complicated
doesn't mean it is.